How To Do Virtualization

Your Step By Step Guide To Virtualization

HowExpert

For more tips related to this topic, visit HowExpert.com/virtualization.

Recommended Resources

- HowExpert.com – Quick 'How To' Guides on All Topics from A to Z by Everyday Experts.
- HowExpert.com/free – Free HowExpert Email Newsletter.
- HowExpert.com/books – HowExpert Books
- HowExpert.com/courses – HowExpert Courses
- HowExpert.com/clothing – HowExpert Clothing
- HowExpert.com/membership – HowExpert Membership Site
- HowExpert.com/affiliates – HowExpert Affiliate Program
- HowExpert.com/writers – Write About Your #1 Passion/Knowledge/Expertise & Become a HowExpert Author.
- HowExpert.com/resources – Additional HowExpert Recommended Resources
- YouTube.com/HowExpert – Subscribe to HowExpert YouTube.
- Instagram.com/HowExpert – Follow HowExpert on Instagram.
- Facebook.com/HowExpert – Follow HowExpert on Facebook.

Publisher's Foreword

Dear HowExpert reader,

HowExpert publishes quick 'how to' guides on all topics from A to Z by everyday experts.

At HowExpert, our mission is to discover, empower, and maximize talents of everyday people to ultimately make a positive impact in the world for all topics from A to Z...one everyday expert at a time!

All of our HowExpert guides are written by everyday people just like you and me who have a passion, knowledge, and expertise for a specific topic.

We take great pride in selecting everyday experts who have a passion, great writing skills, and knowledge about a topic that they love to be able to teach you about the topic you are also passionate about and eager to learn about.

We hope you get a lot of value from our HowExpert guides and it can make a positive impact in your life in some kind of way. All of our readers including you altogether help us continue living our mission of making a positive impact in the world for all spheres of influences from A to Z.

If you enjoyed one of our HowExpert guides, then please take a moment to send us your feedback from wherever you got this book.

Thank you and we wish you all the best in all aspects of life.

Sincerely,

BJ Min
Founder & Publisher of HowExpert
HowExpert.com

PS...If you are also interested in becoming a HowExpert author, then please visit our website at HowExpert.com/writers. Thank you & again, all the best!

Table of Contents

5

Section I: Virtualization

Introduction

Virtualization is the process of creating a virtual version of Network resources. The Network resources could be an Operating system, a server, or external storage device.

Virtualization allows you to run two or more computing environments on two or more operating systems and applications in a cost-effective virtual way. This means you can have a Microsoft OS and Linux or Unix OS in one system or you can have those same applications running on two different OS.

How Virtualization Works

On a physical machine, only one operating system controls the computer's hardware resources; such as CPU, memory, hard disks, system drivers, network drivers etc. at a time.

Since, at a given point of time only one operating system can control the hardware, you can't run more than one operating systems on the same computer at same the time.

How do you get rid of this problem? This is where the concept of Virtualization comes in. Virtual machine technology works like a layer between the computer's physical hardware resources and its operating system.

Each virtual machine has its own dedicated hardware and uses physical resources from its host to run. The host machine still controls the physical hardware.

This results in the hardware of the physical computer being split to serve the host operating system and a number of virtual machines at the same time. It's a very efficient way compartmentalize hardware functions and save space.

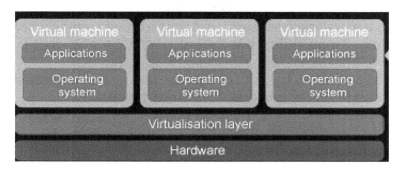

How Virtualization Benefits You

How will virtualization benefit you? Why do you need Virtualization? For today's complex and huge corporate environments, Virtualization provides a number of advantages for IT focused professionals and managers.

Benefits of Virtualization:

- Save Money
- Save Time
- Save Energy

- Save Floor Space
- Reduce and simplify Administrative Desktop Management tasks.
- Resolve Security Issues
- Improve Hardware Utilization

Save Money: Corporate Companies tend to run just one application per server because they don't want to risk the likelihood that if one application crashes, it may bring other apps on the same machine to crash. In a worst-case scenario, a domino effect could cause catastrophic failures in the entire system.

Virtualization helps to overcome this problem because a single server hosts various multi-tasking applications. It also helps to reduce total data center hosting costs, which could be as much as 20% of a business's expenses.

Save Energy: With more servers in utilization for hungry hardware centric applications, businesses spend lots of money on electricity to maintain and cool these servers.

Virtualization minimizes the number of physical servers in utilization, thus reducing energy consumption.

Save Time: Deployment, installation, and maintenance of a server is a major time consideration for major companies. Once the server is operational, performing various server tasks such as backups, restoring, and archiving considerably taxes a System Administrator's time.

With Virtualization, it is easier and faster to deploy a virtual machine and perform the above tasks simultaneously.

Save Floor Space: Virtualization reduces the number of servers hosted in data centers thus reducing necessary physical floor space and saves companies even more money.

Simplified Management Tasks: If a company has a large number of desktops and servers, it would be a tedious job for IT staff to manage, apply hotfixes and patches, and upgrade and secure network resources. It requires in-depth planning and implementation.

Desktop virtualization helps manage desktops and servers in a central virtual location, thus making it feasible to keep desktops and servers in good running order all the time.

Resolve Security Issues: Virtualized systems can reside on the same physical server and thus resolve the issue of providing firewall, proxy configuration. Since some Operating Systems reject external firewall programs, this could become quite a hassle for business owners. With Virtualization, the need for extra firewalls is eliminated.

Improved Hardware Utilization: With virtualization, the CPU utilization increases to 70%, and in some cases 80%, compared to the normal 5-10%.

Testing and Training: Virtualized environments reduce the cost of testing and training because there's no need to retrain or test new servers. Therefore, the company will save wages and man hours that would have been spent on testing and training.

Types of Virtualization

In addition to the desktop virtualization we have other types of virtualization;

- Desktop Virtualization
- Server Virtualization
- Storage Virtualization
- Network Virtualization
- Application Virtualization

Desktop Virtualization: Desktop virtualization provides a way for you to remotely manage individual desktops from a centralized server. This helps IT people to patch, upgrade, and manage their desktops virtually.

We can access the virtualized desktop from various devices such as thin clients, PDAs, laptop computers, tablets, etc.

- **How Desktop virtualization works**
  o Desktop virtualization eliminates the necessity to build additional data centers.
  o It enables desktop disaster recovery.

Server Virtualization: Through server virtualization, a number of operating systems can be run on a single physical machine at same time. Use server virtualization to maximize the utilization of hardware and its resources.

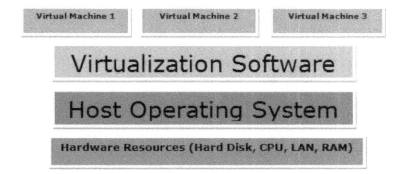

- **How Server virtualization works**
  - o Server virtualization provides the ability to host multiple guest operating systems on a single host server.
  - o The virtualization tools help to supervise different hosts, virtual machines, and data centers simultaneously.

Storage Virtualization: Storage virtualization lets IT staff unite multiple network storage resources to emerge as a single storage device for easier, faster, and more efficient management.

- **How Storage virtualization works**
  - o Storage virtualization tools and software create a logical layer between operating systems and storage on physical disks.
  - o The virtual logical space is then used to manage storage volumes independent of storage location.

- o Storage virtualization supports replication between various storage systems.
- o It also supports live migration, which will be useful if the storage system is offline or in maintenance mode.

Network Virtualization: With network virtualization, the available bandwidth in a network can be split and assigned to various network resources such as servers and devices.

- **How Network virtualization works**
  - o The entire client-server-based network model can be used for network virtualization.
  - o This means routers and switches can now perform more services.
  - o More network applications are moved into network devices.

Application Virtualization: It virtualizes applications that reside in a container without affecting other applications. Application virtualization eliminates conflicts between two applications on the same machine and separates applications from hardware and OS.

Some benefits of using application virtualization are cost reduction on software licenses, efficient hardware utilization, and optimal resource allocation.

- **How Application virtualization works**
  - o Application virtualization virtualizes the file, registry and windows settings environment.

- Applications will run as native window processes within the OS.
- When an application needs the files and registry, the virtualization system intercepts the request within the virtual boundary and processes it.
- This eliminates conflicts between the two applications and DLL hell as each application will reside in its own virtual container.
- For virtual applications to work, each physical computer has to have the virtual client installed.

Section II: How to Build Virtual Machines

Virtualize Desktop Environment

The next step is to virtualize the machine. The virtual machine (VM) can be hosted on a single machine and remain completely isolated from the host machine. All the configuration changes are saved to a single file.

It will be easier to then copy or move the configuration file and host the virtual machine on another host. One more advantage is if one virtual machine crashes, it will not affect other virtual machines or the physical machine.

The first step to a virtual desktop and application is to look at the various solutions that are available in the market and decide which solution would suit you as per your requirement. Some tools are free to use with limited functionality, some are licensed, and some tools bundle with different OS.

These tools provide the most cost efficient and energy efficient data center solutions. Let's look at some of the leading solutions available today.

What Parameters You Should Pay Attention To

The next step is to take care of the following configuration parameters while creating and defining your virtual machines. These parameters would remain the same for all the virtual technologies available.

- **Virtual Machine Name:** This is the name that will be allocated to the virtual machine. The naming convention should reflect the naming methodology that is required in your environment.
- **Processor Allocation:** This refers to the number of virtual processors that need to be allocated to the virtual machine. You need to be aware of how many operating systems and applications the virtual machines will host and the processor capacity of the physical server in order to allocate enough processors to virtual machines.
- **Memory Allocation:** This stands for the amount of memory that needs to be allocated to virtual each machine.
  Again, you need to keep track of how many operating systems and applications the virtual machines host and the physical RAM on the server before allocating memory to virtual machines.
- **Virtual Hard Disk Size:** This represents the memory size necessary for the new IDE based virtual disks.

- **Virtual Disk Location:** If you are connecting to a preexisting virtual machine then you need to provide a location where the files are stored.
- **Virtual Network Connection:** This refers to the type of virtual network connection that you can provide to virtual machines. If the machine is isolated to one machine, you can choose not to use a virtual network adapter.
- **Installation Media:** This gives you the option to install guest virtual operating systems. The installation media could be a bootable CD/DVD media, an ISO image file that contains bootable images, or a virtual floppy boot disk image.
- **Installation Type:** Depending upon what installation media is available to you; you can choose between different installation type.

VMware

VMware is the market leader in virtualization technology. They offer free ESXi and full ESX version products with features like vCenter and vMotion.

vCenter is the centralized tool for managing multiple virtual machine servers. vMotion offers dynamic migration and clustering features. In an upcoming section we will show you how to build a virtualized machine using VMware.

How VMware Virtualization works:

- Download the VMware ESXi application or VMware workstation application.
- Install the software on the physical machine.
- Create a new Virtual Machine (Creating a Virtual Machine will also be covered in an upcoming section).
- VMware creates a thin coating of software on the physical machine hardware or on the operating system.
- This layer of software then can be used to create a fully functional Virtual Machine with its own operating system and applications.
- Each Virtual Machine acts like a real computer and resides within that VMware coating software boundary, which eliminates conflicts between other virtual machines.
- The Virtual Machine then uses the entire system resources such as CPU, operating system, memory, device drives, network drivers etc.
- We can then create multiple Virtual Machines on the same physical machine with each Virtual Machine running different operating systems and applications.

Step-by-Step Action Steps

Let's do a quick step-by-step configuration on creating your own virtual machine using the VMware tool.

1) Once you installed the VMware software, open the VMware workstation link. Then click on File->New->Virtual Machine

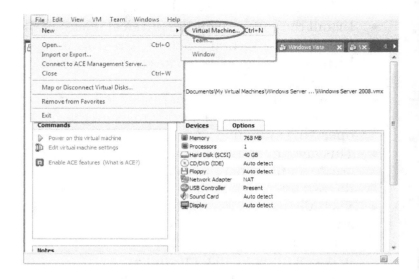

2) Choose the custom option and click next

Note: Custom option is for advanced users and will provide you the various hardware configurations to choose from.

3) Leave the default setting on the next screen and click next

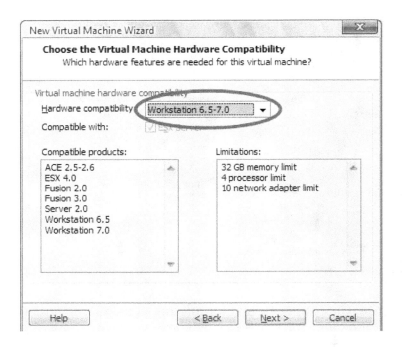

Tips: Choose the latest hardware compatibility option to leverage the maximum benefit as it supports multiple products and large hardware.

4) Choose how you want to install the OS for the virtual machine. The OS can be installed from a bootable CD/DVD or from an ISO file. Browse and choose the ISO for an OS and click next

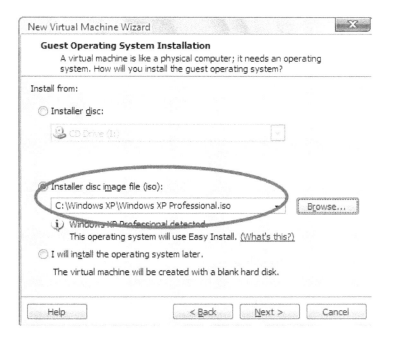

5) Select the product key, name and password. Click next to continue

Note: The product key can be entered later after virtual OS installation is done. If you wish, you can leave the field blank.

6) Enter the virtual machine name and select the location where you need to copy the virtual machine files. Once done, click next

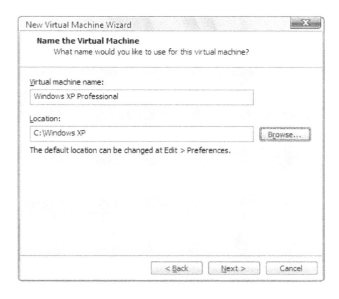

7) Select the number of processors to be used for the virtual machine depending upon your hardware configuration and what types of applications you need to host on it. Click on Next

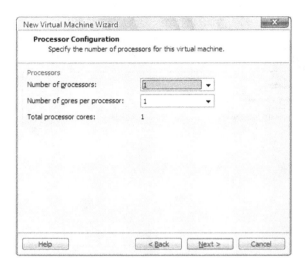

8) Select how much memory is to be used. The minimum recommended is 512 MB.

Click Next to proceed.

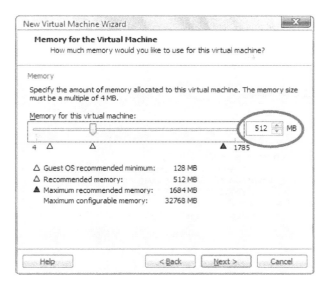

Tips: The memory selection depends on how much RAM is available on your physical machine and what types of applications are to be hosted on the virtual machine.

9) Choose your network type on next installation screen. If the virtual machine is to be used on the corporate network then use the bridged networking option else use NAT.

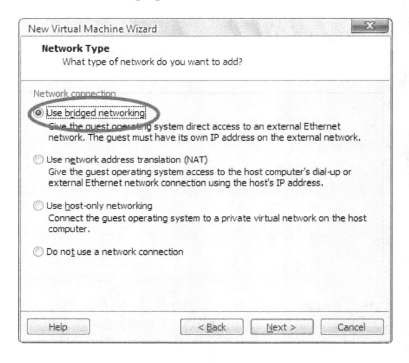

10) Select the type of adapter and click next

11) Since we are creating a new virtual machine for this walkthrough, select create a new virtual disk option and click next.

12) On the next screen, select a disk type and click next

13) Choose the disk space size that needs to be allocated (recommended is 40 GB). Also select whether the virtual machine configuration file will be store in a single file or can be splits into 2GB file each.

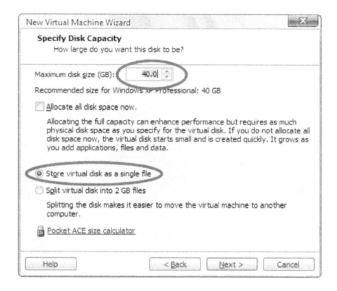

14) Specify a file name. The file name is stored as a .vmdk extension. Do not erase the extension. A missing file extension will cause your computer to fail to find the file later. Click next to continue installation.

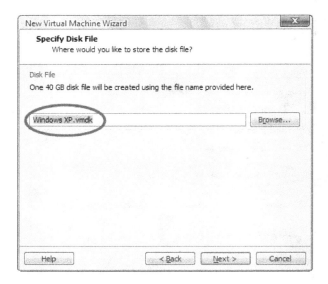

15) The next screen will provide you the summary of selection that is chosen for installation. Put a check mark on power on this virtual machine to start the Virtual machine after creation is over.

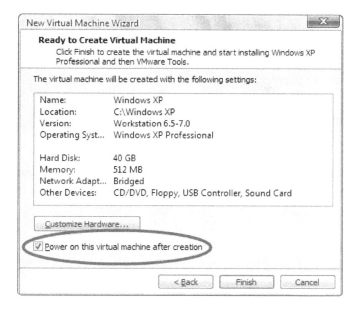

31

16) The OS installation will then start.

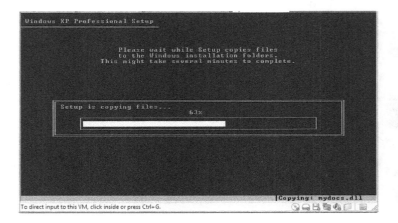

After OS installation is done you are ready to login to the virtual machine and start working on it. We can host multiple virtual Operating systems using the same process on the same physical machine.

17) To power on any virtual machine, highlight the OS which needs to be powered and select the "Power on this virtual machine" option.

Citrix XenServer

Citrix XenServer is the virtualization tool that provides cloud server virtualization, live migration, centralized multi server management, and virtual infrastructure patch management solutions.

Step-by-Step Action Steps

- Download XenServer and XenCenter management console tools.
- Install the software on the physical machine.
- Add a server to the XenServer.
- Activate the license from the Citrix server to proceed creating a new virtual machine.
- Create a new Virtual Machine with easy to follow steps using XenCenter's guide that should pop up.
- Use the built-in features of XenServer to manage your Virtual Machines environment.

Let's compare the VMware and Citrix XenServer free tools and the features available on them.

Features	Citrix XenServer	VMware ESXI
Multiple OS hosting	Available	Available
Unlimited server hosts	Available	Available
Shared storage (SAN, NAS)	Available	Available
Centralized Management	Available	Not Available
Live Motion	Available	Not Available

Patch Management	Available	Not Available
Server Maintenance mode	Available	Not Available

Microsoft Virtual PC

Microsoft Virtual PC is a free download tool from Microsoft. Like other virtualization tools, Virtual PC creates a work space or layer on which another operating system can run.

Virtual PC will run most of the operating platforms including Microsoft and non-Microsoft operating system.

How Virtual PC Virtualization works:

- Download the Virtual PC application from Microsoft.
- Install the application onto the physical machine.
- Create a new virtual machine using a virtual PC image.
- The image file is a vhd extension which contains all the configuration information of the virtual operating system.

- The hardware resources allocated to the vhd file is managed by a file with vmc extension.
- The vmc file manages memory, network, and system resources information.

Step-by-Step Action Steps

We will now create a virtual machine using Virtual PC.

1) Launch the Virtual PC application. Click on file->New to start the new virtual machine wizard.

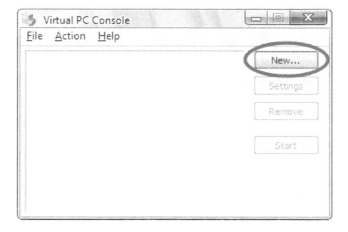

2) On the wizard click next to continue

3) Choose the option to create a new virtual machine

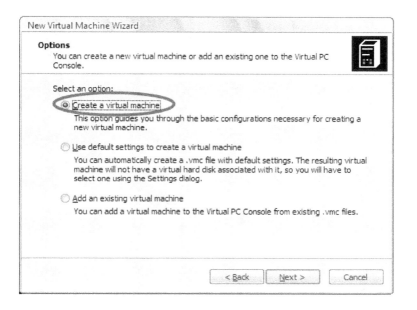

4) Provide a name and location where you need to keep the configuration files. Click on next

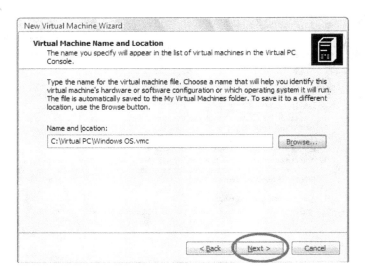

5) Select an operating system for the Virtual PC from the operating system drop down menu and click next

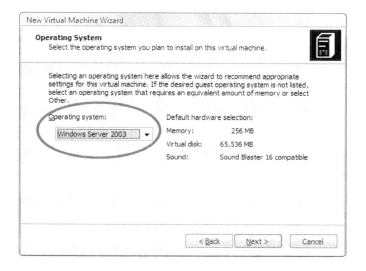

41

6) Select the recommended RAM option or choose how much RAM can be allocated to this Virtual PC by selecting and adjusting the RAM option. Then click next to continue

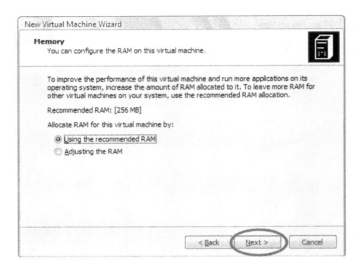

7) Select the option 'a new virtual hard disk' and click next

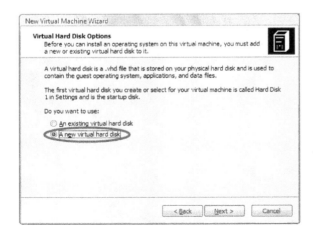

8) Provide virtual hard disk space for the new virtual machine and click next

9) Click finish to complete the new virtual machine wizard.

10) The virtual PC will now be listed as one of the PCs on the Virtual PC console.

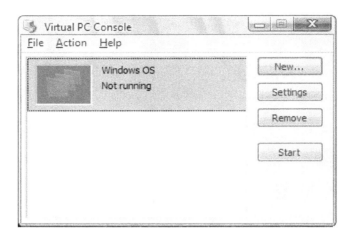

11) The settings that we have done while creating the machine can be further re-customized. Select the virtual machine and click on settings.

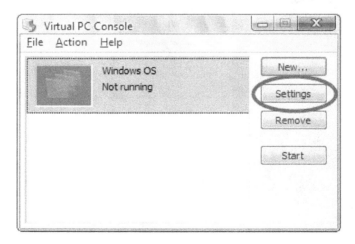

12) The settings wizard will help you select various system resources for the virtual PC.

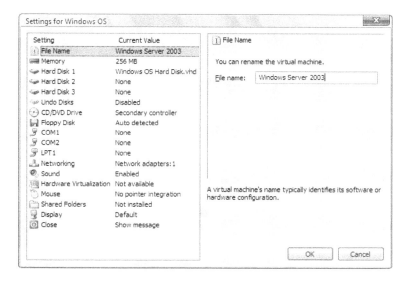

13) At this point the virtual machine is in 'not running' mode. Click on start to run the virtual machine.

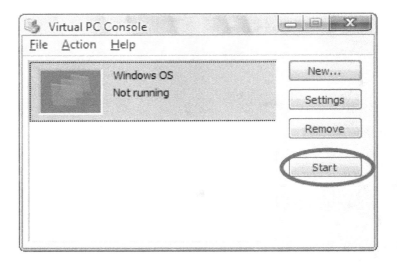

To Do: make sure you have the bootable CD/DVD inserted into CD/Drive drive before starting the virtual PC. Virtual PC will load the operating system installation files from here and will start installing operating system.

Section III: How to Build Virtual Application

Create a New Virtual Application

Now that we have virtual machines and know how to create them, your next step is to create a new virtual sequencing application. The most popular tool for sequencing applications is Microsoft Application Virtualization (App-V) sequencer.

Microsoft App-V

Microsoft Application Virtualization (App-V) provides a customizable way of using an application on a desktop or terminal machine without installing an application to the user's OS. The application resides in an isolated virtual environment on the host client.

Now we will go over some of the terminology used for application virtualization processes that are commonly used for all the tools.

Application Virtualization Terminology:

- Application Sequencing
- Application Streaming
- Model
- Client

Application Sequencing: The implementation and creation of virtual applications through certain steps is called sequencing. The sequencing tool should be installed on a clean machine and it is best to use a virtual machine for this purpose.

Application Streaming: Application streaming provides software use on demand services.

Whenever the user launches an application (by clicking on the shortcut), the software gets downloaded to the user's machine from server.

Streaming provides a reduction on licensing of products as the products will not get installed on all user machines.

Model: How an application is virtualized and how it is published and deploy to the end user is defined through a process called Model. We have 3 types of models to support virtualization.

A. Standalone Model: We can create a MSI based virtual application without streaming using standalone model.
B. Streaming Model: With the streaming model, virtual applications can be streamed, deployed, and distributed via deployment tools (like SMS, SCCM). It works without an AD and Database infrastructure in place.
C. Full Infrastructure Model: This is an advanced model that provides streaming, built-in deployment, and reporting facility.

Client: This is the end user machine that runs the virtual applications. The client takes care of the streaming and downloads the software from server to its local cache.

An application sequence is done in 4 different steps viz. Installation, Launch, Customization and Save. Below is the graphical view of the 4 stages and processes and operations for each step that we need to follow.

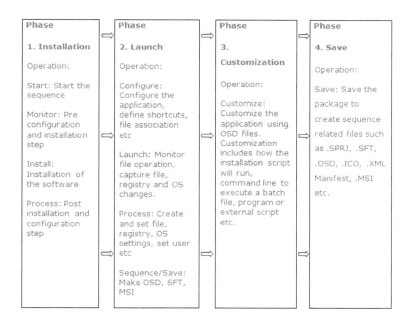

The file details are explained below.

- OSD file: This is the main configuration sequencer file and contains package location information, dependencies information, scripts, shell integration and package environment information.

- SPRJ file: Sequencing project file that has package settings, exclusion and configuration items.
- SFT file: SFT file contains streaming feature blocks information with its assets and state information.
- ICO file: Icon file link to each shortcut in the virtual package. The information is also stored in the OSD file.
- XML Manifest: It has information of shortcuts, DDE, shell integration definition information.
- MSI file: Installer file used in case of standalone model environments.

Let's install and configure step-by-step installation and configuration of App-V sequencer and perform sequencing for a sample application.

Steps for Installing Sequencer

1) Run the sequencer installer executable file setup.exe. On the welcome screen click next to continue

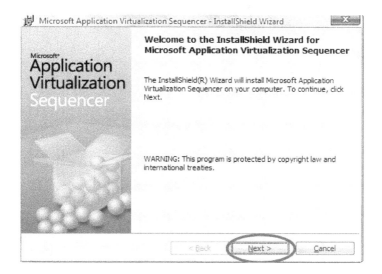

2) Select I accept the terms on the license agreement page and click next

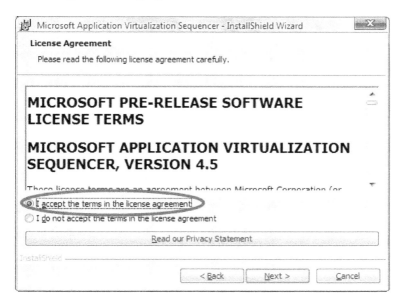

3) Leave the default installation folder and click next to continue installation

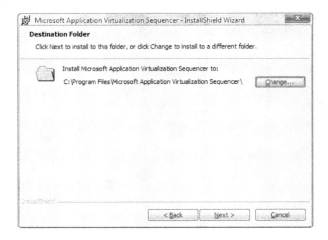

4) The installation wizard is now ready to install sequencer, click Install

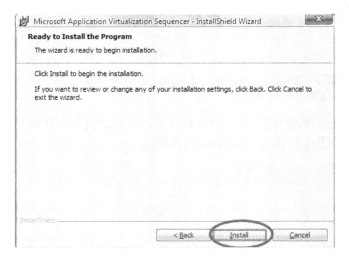

5) When installation is done click Finish to complete the installation

Steps for Sequencing a Package:

The next step is to create a package and go through all the sequencing processes, namely installation, launch, customization, and save.

The recommended prerequisite is to create two partitions in the machine. One partition would be C: where OS is installed and other partition is Q: used for the destination directory for package installation.

1) Start the Application Virtualization Sequence shortcut. On the package menu, select create a new package option. Enter a package name, enter a comment and put a check on Show Advanced Monitoring options.

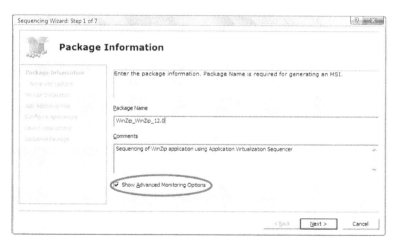

Note: Microsoft recommended to use <Appname>_<AppVendor>_<Version>_<MNT/VFS) package naming convention. If you are installing application to C:\ drive provide VFS and for Q: drive installation provides MNT.

2) Leave the default option and select next

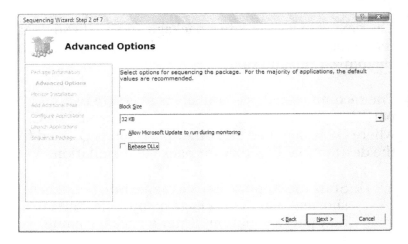

Note: Allow Microsoft update option needs to be checked when you need to update the application during package installation (e.g. Microsoft office application)

Rebase DLLs option is used for terminal server installation where the DLLs are mapped to a continuous series in RAM.

Click on Begin Monitoring button to start monitoring installation of the package.

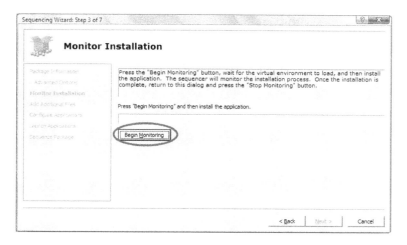

3) The installation will then prompt you to choose an installation directory where the sequence will store monitoring activity.

4) The monitoring process will start. The wizard will guide you to begin installation of the package. Install your package and once done click on stop monitoring.

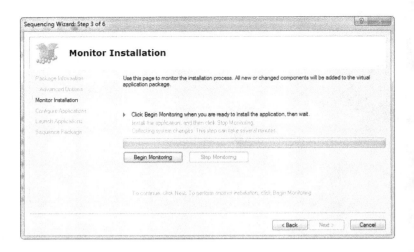

Note: Some applications may require a reboot for complete installation. Since we are creating a virtual application, we need not to restart the physical machine just yet.

5) For applications that require a reboot, start the 'begin monitoring' process and install the application. When it prompts for reboot, select 'stop monitoring' and then again select 'begin monitoring'. Sequence will keep track of the changes and process them to include in the package.

6) The next process is to configure the application. We can configure which shortcuts and file associations are needed for this application.

There is also an option to add shortcuts and file association which is not listed by the capturing wizard.

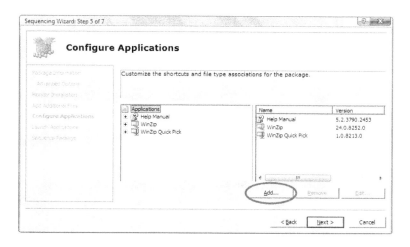

7) The next step is to launch all the applications. This ensures the package is optimized for streaming for the subsequent frequent use.

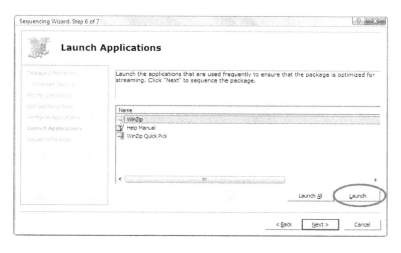

Tips: It is a good practice to launch all the applications so that sequence will capture all the required settings. This will allow you to immediately check your parameters and make any adjustments necessary.

8) Click on next to launch all the applications. The sequencer wizard will close and package deployment wizard will appear.

Once sequencing is complete, the package can then further be configured using package deployment wizard.

9) Click on deployment tab. It will provide you the option to choose different operating system environments. There is also an option to create a MSI package (for standalone installation)

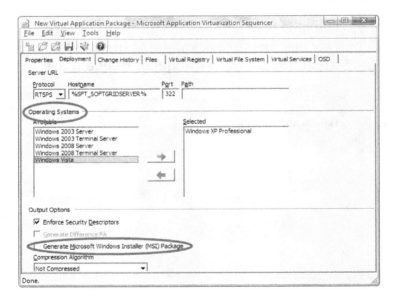

10) The last step is to save the package. This will create sprj file. Choose file and click on Save.

Conclusion

Virtualization technologies are growing day by day as today's corporations are opting for reduction in their total cost of ownership (TCO).

Virtualization reduces the cost of hosting and managing servers. It helps to reduce power consumption, noise and heat generation, and floor space occupied by physical servers.

Virtualization allows entire networks and applications to be reconfigured to meet today's demand in a simplified way.

Further network virtualization increases the flexibility of creating multiple networks to support both virtual and physical traffic. More and more virtualized server operating systems and applications can be managed while remaining independent of physical hardware.

With application virtualization, enterprises are finding it easy to manage and update their legacy applications. It is also helping them to ease the difficulties of deploying complicated desktop configurations.

Effective virtualization planning and designing will increase overall flexibility of IT which will result in higher delivering capabilities.

Virtualization is evolving on a daily basis to keep up with ever-changing technologies. With its cost saving capabilities, Virtualization is here to stay.

Recommended Resources

- HowExpert.com – Quick 'How To' Guides on All Topics from A to Z by Everyday Experts.
- HowExpert.com/free – Free HowExpert Email Newsletter.
- HowExpert.com/books – HowExpert Books
- HowExpert.com/courses – HowExpert Courses
- HowExpert.com/clothing – HowExpert Clothing
- HowExpert.com/membership – HowExpert Membership Site
- HowExpert.com/affiliates – HowExpert Affiliate Program
- HowExpert.com/writers – Write About Your #1 Passion/Knowledge/Expertise & Become a HowExpert Author.
- HowExpert.com/resources – Additional HowExpert Recommended Resources
- YouTube.com/HowExpert – Subscribe to HowExpert YouTube.
- Instagram.com/HowExpert – Follow HowExpert on Instagram.
- Facebook.com/HowExpert – Follow HowExpert on Facebook.